i love knitting

i love knitting

25 LOOPY PROJECTS THAT WILL SHOW YOU HOW TO KNIT EASILY AND QUICKLY

RACHEL HENDERSON

PHOTOGRAPHY BY KATE WHITAKER

ST. MARTIN'S GRIFFIN
NEW YORK

This edition published in 2006 by St Martin's Press
175 Fifth Avenue, New York, N.Y. 10010

First published in Great Britain in 2006 by Kyle Cathie

ISBN-13: 978-0-312-36941-5
ISBN-10: 0-312-36941-7

Editorial director: Muna Reyal
Art direction and design by Jenny Semple
Photography by Kate Whitaker
Styling by Penny Markham
Artwork by Roberta Boyce
Pattern checking by Penny Hill
Copyediting by Kate Haxell
Production: Sha Huxtable and Alice Holloway
Americaniser: Sally MacEchern
Models: Amy Redmond, Jacob Love, Laura Wheatley, Jenny Wheatley

Rachel Henderson is hereby identified as the author of this work in accordance with Section 77 of the Copyright,
Designs and Patents Act 1988.

The Library of Congress Cataloging-in-Publication Data is available on file

Color reproduction by Sang Choy
Printed in Singapore by Star Standard

contents

my knitted world

My story is different. People tend to expect me to say "Yeah… I've been knitting since I was five years old," but actually it wasn't until I was in my final year of my textile degree that I got the knitting vibe, and a rather addictive strain at that.

I'll always remember my first visit to my local notions store. There I was, a typical art student and a wool virgin, getting as excited about the yarn and patterns as I had been about buying my favorite indie band's new album—how could this be? It was then that I realized I was a knitaholic and my obsession with knitting has grown ever since.

going nuts

But when I first started out, I found myself, like many other beginners, driven to distraction by the jargon used in knitting patterns. Now I'm a consultant in hand knitting and I still hear the words, "it's like a foreign language" muttered by beginner knitters as they dive into their first pattern, their eagerness soon clouded over, quashed by the liberal use of knitting slang. So this book is as jargon-free as I can make it.

Patience is the key, my grandmother used to say when I manically chucked her thin needles and skinny 2-ply yarn in the air, eager to learn the basics, but frustrated at how fussy it seemed. Patience is something that is becoming more and more unfamiliar as our lives get busier, and sitting down to create something seems almost impossible. But I want to change this.

I want to show you that anyone can knit. That you can knit anywhere (have a look at my extreme knitting photos). And that you can knit something that you might actually want to wear. Or give to somebody. I want to bring out the designer in you. And when you need a break from those noisy needles, I will also show you a few other things you can do with your needles and wool.

customizing designs

Once you have mastered the techniques chapter, got yourself a good gauge and followed a few of my patterns without getting too tied up in knots, I want you to take a stab at my inspirational chapter, "Customizing Designs." At my knitting circle I'm constantly seeing young girls coming up with their own knitted

designs, so in order to inspire you, I asked five of my creative friends to come up with a design based on their skills and background. Whether you try Amy's felted flower, Di's knitted panty, Louise's funky cuff, Suzie's evening purse or Kate's painted tote bag, I'm hoping that after having a try at one or two of these projects, you will be inspired enough to create your very own knitted designs.

Knitting is such a versatile craft, and customizing it is a great way to awaken your creative soul. By changing yarn, adding beads, or embroidering, you can create a one-off piece that is personal to you. That's also why I haven't specified colors for each project— I want to bring out the designer in you and choosing the color combinations you like is a great way to start.

When I was working on projects at art college, I remember being so excited to see the end results, and to discuss with each other what our inspiration was and how we got there. Each person's design always differed, whether through color, shape, the materials they used, or what they were inspired by. Their personalities and favorite skills were literally woven into their projects.

That's what made this book great to work on—it made me feel like a student again. I had almost forgotten how much fun it used to be and I want to pass this excitement onto you.

So I hope that this chapter, Customizing Designs, along with the rest of the book, will give you the confidence to start designing. Just pick out some colors and yarns and create your own patterns. Anyone can be a designer and the possibilities are endless. If they can do it, you can too!

knitting and talking

Nowadays knitting is seen as a "cool" thing to do, a good way of filling time, whether you're in a café, in front of the TV, or sitting on a train. It is also really sociable and portable— more and more people just take their needles wherever they go, letting their hands work on while they talk to their friends, watch a movie, or just let their mind relax and wander.

Knitting is great! And that comes straight from the horse's mouth!

After my first book *Pub Knitting*, I wanted to use the same light-hearted approach to knitting. I have come up with fun designs that I hope you will be able to follow without tying yourself up in knots. They won't take too long to knit nor use lots of yarn or complicated techniques, so I hope that you will have lots of fun with it.

This book is called *I Love Knitting* because that's why I wrote it, and that's the way it should be…

Rachel x

how to knit

I'll begin this section by saying that knitting is easier than it looks, even if you're not a naturally creative person and you think that you have big clumsy hands. All those fussy-looking techniques often put people off, but if you treat learning to knit like any other skill you've embarked on in the past, you'll find that once you've grasped the basics anything is possible and after a few months you will no doubt be addicted!

What you will need (p15)

Super bulky yarn | Soft bulky yarn with ribbon | Supersoft tweed aran mix | Chunky textured yarn

getting started

There is no right or wrong way to hold your needles. Once you start knitting, you will soon find the most comfortable position for you. In the UK and the US, the yarn is usually held in the right hand (see step 5 on page 20), but in Europe, it is often held in the left hand (see below right). Whichever hand you use, it will control the gauge of your yarn, i.e. how tightly you hold it.

HOW TO HOLD THE NEEDLES

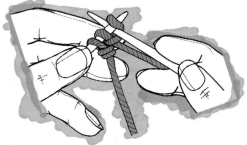

I hold my needles between my thumb and index finger.

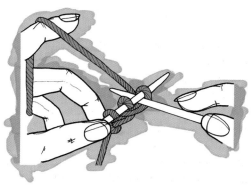

In Europe, the needles and yarn are held like this.

Double knitting cotton   Double knitting cashmire mix   Mercerized cotton   Super kid light mohair and silk

CHOOSING A YARN AND NEEDLES

There are so many different types of yarns on the market today and this can make it confusing to know exactly what yarn you should choose, taking into account the type of project you are making.

The three factors you should take into account when choosing a yarn are weight (or thickness), composition (what it's made of), and length.

Weight This is based on the number of plies (or strands) the yarn is made up of. The thinnest yarn is 2-ply and it goes up in size through fine, light, medium, and bulky to extra-bulky.

Composition Yarns are made up of many different fibers, from natural ones such as merino wool, alpaca, silk, cotton, and linen to artificial ones such as nylon, acrylic, and viscose. The yarn's ball band will always tell you what the yarn is made of and also give you washing information.

Length The yardage of yarn in a ball can vary, even if the yarns are the same type and the balls weigh the same. It is the yardage that is vital, so if you are using a different yarn to the one in a pattern, check the ball band for the yardage and make sure you buy enough.

Like wool, needles also come in various materials—metal, plastic, bamboo, and wood. All of them will give the same results, but some people prefer bamboo needles because they are lighter and can be easier to work with, while others prefer metal or plastic. At the end of the day, it's what works best for you.

Needles also come in different sizes and lengths and your choice of needle will usually be based on the weight of yarn you will be using—the ball band will give you recommendations. The length of the needle will depend on the project you are working on (i.e. if you need to cast on a large number of stitches, then choose a long pair of needles). Using bulky yarn on thick needles will mean your knitting grows quickly.

A knitting pattern will always tell you what type of yarn to use and what size of needle. If you want to choose a different yarn from that suggested, the important thing to do is to match the gauge to the one given in the pattern. A suggested gauge will usually be shown on the ball band.

equipment

To be honest, all you really need is a pair of needles and some yarn, but as with anything, you can buy as much or as little equipment as you like. Here are a few things that will ease your knitted life.

1 Tape measure: This is a handy thing to have, especially when checking your gauge square at the beginning of a project.

2 Knitter's sewing or darning needles: These are essential for darning in ends and sewing up your project. If you are using a very bulky yarn, make sure that it will fit through the eye of your needle.

3 Scissors: A small pair of scissors is always useful for trimming ends of yarns.

4 Flower head pins: When you are sewing up your project, you will find them helpful in keeping the fabric in place.

5 Bobbins: When working with different colors in a project these are really handy to have. They will help keep the different yarns from tangling and speed up the process of knitting with color.

6 Notepad and pen: This is always good to have on hand, especially if you are designing a new project, or just need to keep count of your rows and stitches when working on a project.

7 Knitter's graph paper: Good to have if you want to create your own knitted motif (see page 37).

8 Stitch counter: If you hang one on the end of each needle, it will help you keep count of what row you are on. If you have only one counter, remember to count two rows each time.

9 Crochet hook: Useful for tweaking stitches or picking up dropped ones, as well as adding a fringe to a scarf, for example

10 Cable needles: Used in cable knitting (see page 38). They come in several different designs, but you will soon find out which one suits you best.

gauge

You will always hear the word "gauge" in a conversation about knitting. It's the number one word in any knitter's vocabulary, but what does it mean?

Your gauge is how tightly or loosely you knit. Most people don't realize how important it is to get it right until they begin their first project, but it will affect the size of your finished garment or accessory. If you knit tightly your project might end up too small or if you knit loosely it might end up too big.

Always knit a gauge square before you start a project. Use the same needles, yarn, and stitch pattern as the project does.

The knitting pattern you are using will tell you how many stitches and rows you should have to 4in/10cm, so cast on at least 6 more stitches than the number given and knit at least 6 more rows.

MEASURING YOUR GAUGE SQUARE

Lay the square flat on a surface. To count the stitches, lay a tape measure horizontally across the square—with the end a couple of stitches in from the edge—and count the number of stitches to 4in/10cm. To count the rows, do the same thing but lay the tape vertically across the square.

If you have too few stitches, try again with larger needles. If you have too many, use smaller needles. Don't try to knit at a different gauge to that which comes naturally to you; you won't be able to keep it up throughout the project.

how to cast on

This is where it all starts. Casting on is the way of getting the right number of stitches onto your needle to begin your project.

RACHEL'S TIP: When getting started, try holding your needles loosely and don't be afraid of them—if you make a mistake, remember you can always undo the yarn and start all over again.

The cable method works well with stockinette stitch and the thumb method is ideal with garter stitch.

Whether you use the cable or thumb method of casting on, don't pull on the yarn too hard or your cast on will be too tight and it will be hard to knit the first row.

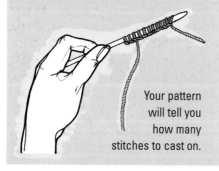

Your pattern will tell you how many stitches to cast on.

CABLE METHOD

This method of casting on gives a firm, strong edging to your knitted fabric.

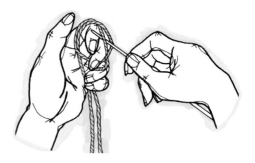

1 Before you cast on your stitches, leave an arm's short tail of yarn and make a slip knot by winding the yarn round twice around two fingers on your left hand, with the second loop behind the first one.

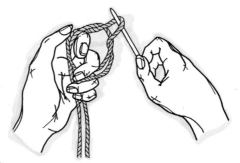

2 With a knitting needle in your right hand, pull the second loop of yarn through the first loop on your fingers.

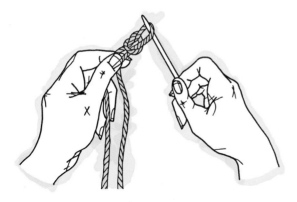

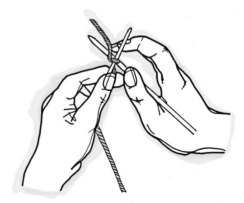

3 Pull both ends of the yarn to tighten the knot. You now have your first cast on stitch. Hold this needle in your left hand.

4 Using the right-hand needle, go through the bottom of the slip knot on the left-hand needle. Then take the main yarn around the back of the right-hand needle and between both needles.

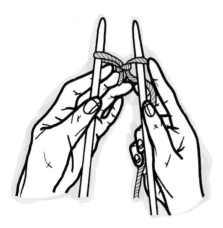

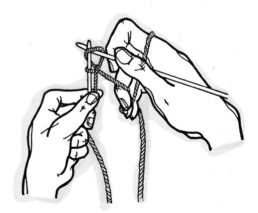

5 Slide the right-hand needle down through the the slip knot on the left-hand needle and under, pulling the yarn lying over the right-hand needle through the loop on the left-hand needle. You should now have a loop on each needle.

6 Slip the loop on the right-hand needle onto the left-hand needle and gently pull the yarn tight. You should now have 2 stitches on the left-hand needle. Working into the first stitch on the left-hand needle, repeat steps 4–6 until you have the required number of cast on stitches (see diagram in box, opposite).

THUMB METHOD

This gives you a more elastic edging to your piece of knitted fabric.

First, follow steps 1–3 of Cable Method, leaving a long yarn tail.

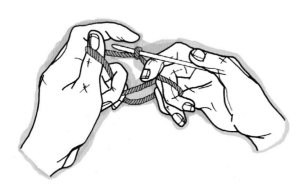

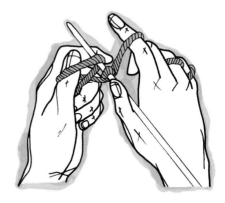

4 You are now going to use the long tail of yarn to cast on all your stitches. Take hold of the tail of yarn with three of your fingers and go over the top and under with your thumb, twisting the yarn around your thumb.

5 Slide the right-hand needle under the bottom of the thumb loop.

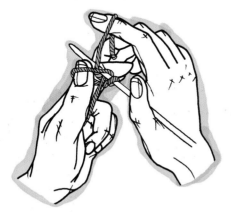

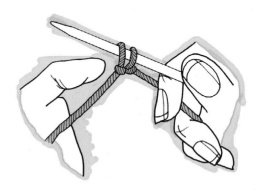

6 Take the main bit of yarn around the back of the needle and lift the thumb loop over the needle.

7 Pull the tail of yarn tight. You should now have 2 cast on stitches on your needle. Repeat steps 4–7 until you have the required number of cast on stitches on your needle.

how to knit (k)

A knit stitch is the most basic type of stitch.

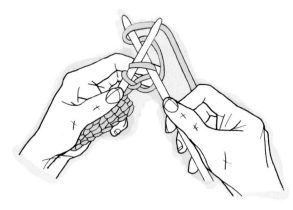

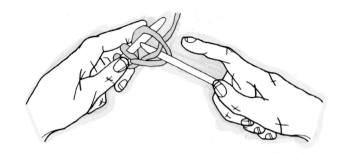

1 With the main working yarn at the back of the work, insert the right-hand needle through the bottom of the first stitch and to the back of the left-hand needle, making a cross with the needles. Take the main working yarn around the back of the right-hand needle and then between both needles.

2 Slide the right-hand needle down through the top of the loop on the left-hand needle and under, pulling the yarn lying over the right-hand needle through the loop. Pull the yarn tight.

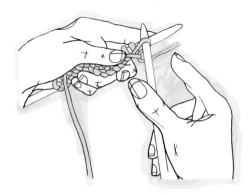

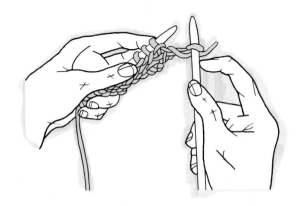

3 Slip the original stitch off the left-hand needle.

4 Repeat these steps until all the stitches on the left needle have been knitted. This is called a row.

how to purl (p)

A purl stitch is the second-most basic type of stitch and is the reverse of the knit stitch.

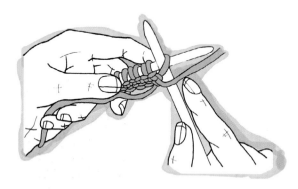

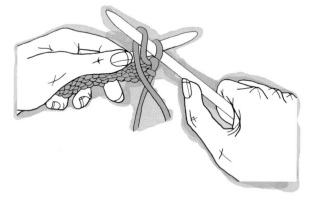

1 With the working yarn at the front of the work, insert the right-hand needle in through the top of the first stitch on the left-hand needle and to the front, making a cross with the needles.

2 Take the main working yarn around the back of the right-hand needle to the front.

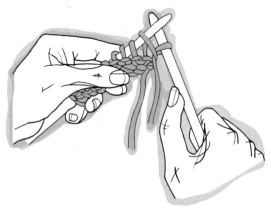

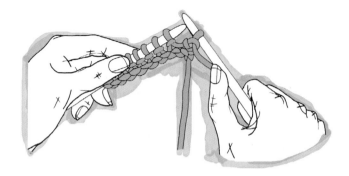

3 Slide the right-hand needle down through the bottom of the loop on the left-hand needle, pulling the yarn through the loop and pull tight.

4 Slip the original stitch off the left-hand needle. Repeat these steps until all the stitches on the left-hand needle have been purled.

how to bind off

Binding off is a very simple process and is done after you have finished your piece of knitting to secure your stitches so they don't unravel.

① First of all, you need to knit 2 stitches.

② Using the left-hand needle, pick up the first knitted stitch on the right-hand needle.

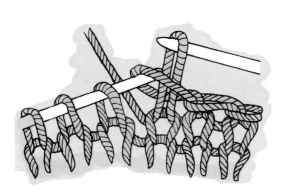

③ Carry this stitch over your second knitted stitch on the right needle and let it drop off the left needle. Knit another stitch and repeat steps 2 and 3.

④ Once you have bound off all your stitches, pass the end of the yarn through the last stitch and pull tightly.

basic stitch patterns

By combining your two basic stitches, knit and purl, you can produce lots of simple knitted textures such as garter, stockinette, seed, and rib.

RACHEL'S TIP: Basic stitch patterns are so much fun to do as they don't take too much time or concentration. Why not combine two of these stitch patterns together and create your own knitted fabric design.

You can then get a bit more experimental and try combining knit and purl stitches in other patterns.

① GARTER STITCH

Garter stitch is the most basic knitted fabric and is produced by simply knitting (or purling) on every single row. This forms a strong and firm pattern of raised horizontal ridges and the knitted fabric will not curl at the edges.

To make garter stitch, cast on any number of stitches and knit every row. You can work garter stitch with every row purl, but this is rarely done.

② STOCKINETTE STITCH

This is probably the most commonly used knitting stitch pattern. The knit stitches on stockinette stitch are referred to as the right side (shown here) and the purl stitches as the wrong side. The purl side is also called the reverse stockinette stitch. This looks similar to a garter stitch, but the ridges are slightly smaller and closer together in reverse stockinette stitch.

To make stockinette stitch, cast on any number of stitches. On the first row knit all the stitches, on the second row, purl all the stitches, and repeat these rows to the end.

③ SEED STITCH

This is one of my favorite stitches. It's not the quickest of stitches as you need to keep lifting the yarn back and forth after each stitch, but it gives a nice firm piece of knitted fabric that doesn't curl at the sides. This fabric is usually created by casting on an odd number of stitches and always beginning and ending with a knit stitch.

To make seed stitch, cast on an uneven number of stitches. On the first row, knit the first stitch, purl the next, and repeat to the end—you will finish on a knit stitch. Do the same for the following rows.

④ RIB STITCH

This fabric is composed of vertical "ribs" of stitches. You can make a rib as big or as small as you want by adjusting the number of stitches you knit and purl on each row.

To make double rib stitch (shown here), cast on a multiple of 4 stitches plus 2 extra. On the first row, knit 2, then purl 2, then knit 2, and repeat to the end. On the 2nd row, begin with 2 purl stitches, then 2 knit stitches. Repeat these 2 rows to the end.

shaping

Increasing and decreasing simply mean adding or reducing the number of stitches. Use these techniques to shape your knitted project.

RACHEL'S TIP: Making a stitch "M1" doesn't show much, so is often used if you want to increase in the middle of a row.

Increasing a stitch "inc 1" shows more as there is a little bar of yarn across the bottom of the new stitch. It's often used on an edge, as the bar will disappear into the seam when the pieces of knitting are sewn together.

"K2tog" (shown overleaf) slants to the right on a knit row, while "p2tog" slants to the left on a purl row. "Skpo" slants to the left on a knit row and is often used at the other end of a row to "k2tog" to produce mirror-image decreases.

INCREASING

Making a stitch (make one "M1")

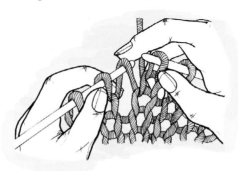

1 Using your left-hand needle, pick up the horizontal strand lying in between both needles.

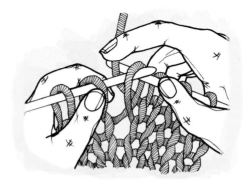

2 Using the right-hand needle, go through the back of the picked-up strand on the left-hand needle and knit it as usual.

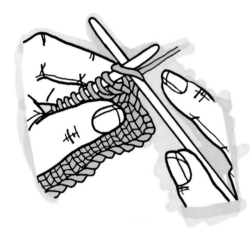

Increasing a stitch (inc 1)

1 Using your right-hand needle, go into the stitch and knit it as usual, but do not slip the original stitch off the left-hand needle.

2 Using the right-hand needle, go through the back of the same stitch and knit the stitch again.

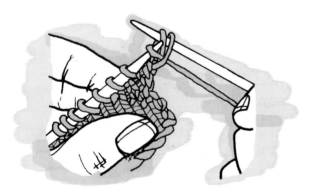

3 Slip the original stitch off the left-hand needle.

DECREASING

Knit 2 together ("k2tog")

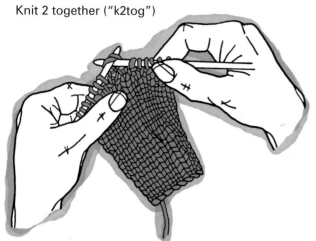

1 On a knit row, using your right-hand needle go through the bottom of the next 2 stitches on your left-hand needle and to the back, and knit them together.

Purl 2 together ("p2tog")

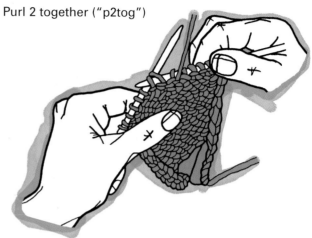

2 On a purl row, using your right-hand needle, go in through the top of the next 2 stitches on your left-hand needle and to the front, and purl them together.

Slip 1, knit 1, pass slipped stitch over ("skpo")

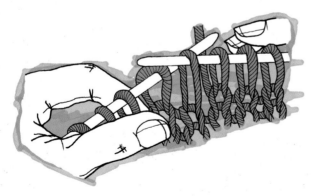

1 Using your right-hand needle, go through the bottom of the next stitch on your left-hand needle and slip it onto your right needle. Knit the next stitch.

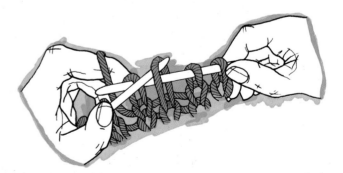

2 Using your left-hand needle, pick up the slipped stitch on your right-hand needle and pass it over your knitted stitch.

finishing

So you've got to the end of the pattern safely and you've bound off your project, but how do you put it together?

RACHEL'S TIP: Before you sew the pieces together you need to darn in any tails of yarn left from casting on and binding off, joining in new balls of yarn, or from color work. Thread a darning needle with the tail and weave the needle through the backs of four or five adjacent stitches, pulling the yarn through. Then weave it back on itself to secure it. Do not pull the yarn too tight or the knitted fabric will pucker.

Take your time sewing up: you put effort into knitting the project, so don't rush now and spoil it.

BACKSTITCH

Backstitch forms a thick, strong, and firm seam and is usually used with lightweight yarns. With this stitch, you are working on the wrong sides of the knitted fabric with the right sides placed together.

Using a darning needle, work ¼in. from the edge of the knitting. Go through the center of a stitch to match it to the same stitch on the other edge, and make each stitch about ½in. long.

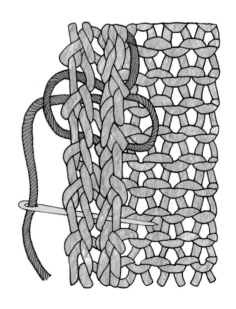

MATTRESS STITCH

Mattress stitch is my favorite way of sewing up as it creates a completely invisible seam, but it can sometimes take a little practice to get right.

With the right sides of the knitting facing you, pick up the first 2 horizontal bars between the first and the second stitches on the left piece of knitting. Now go across to the right piece and pick up the same 2 bars on that piece.

Go back across to the left piece and pick up the next 2 bars in between the stitches and then pick up the same 2 bars on the opposite piece. Continue like this, firmly pulling the yarn to form the seam.

EDGE TO EDGE STITCH

This is the best method to use when knitting with lightweight yarns.

Working with the wrong sides facing you, place both pieces of fabric together, matching them row for row and stitch for stitch. Taking the needle through the head of each stitch, sew the seam up in a zigzag fashion, as shown below.

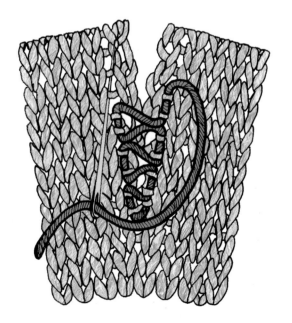

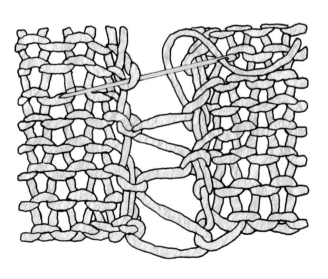

knitting with beads

This is a lovely and very simple decorative method that you can use to make knitted jewelry, change purses, or garments.

RACHEL'S TIP: All you need for this technique are beads, a sewing needle and thread, and yarn.

Before you start to knit with beads, check that the holes in them are big enough for the yarn that you are knitting with.

A pattern will always tell you when to add a bead by saying "B1" or "PB" (place bead).

Always make sure that you pull the yarn firmly after adding a bead so that it is held close against the fabric.

Slide the beads down the yarn as you knit, bringing them up one at a time as you need them.

KNITTING WITH BEADS

Beaded knitting is one of my favorite techniques. I love the way that, just by adding beads to a plain knitted design, you can make it look really glamorous. Beading can take longer than other decorative techniques but it's always worth being patient with.

Before casting on, loop a length of thread around the yarn and thread the ends through a needle.

One at a time, slide the beads down the needle and thread and onto the yarn. The pattern will tell you how many beads to thread on, but I always thread on a few more just to be safe. Push the beads down the yarn a short way and cast on the stitches needed.

ADDING BEADS WITH A SLIP STITCH

Adding beads with a slip stitch is the most common way of beading knitting and it works on both the knit side and the purl side rows. However, you can only add a bead on every other stitch and alternate row. The steps below show how to bead on a knit row. If working a purl row, bring the yarn to the back of the work, and slip the stitch knit-wise.

1 On a knit row, push the next bead up and bring the yarn through between the needles and to the front of the work.

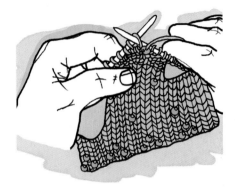

2 Slip the next stitch purl-wise from your left-hand needle onto your right-hand needle.

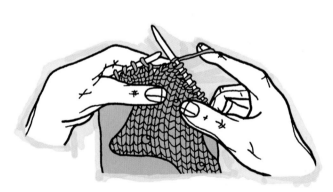

3 Bring the yarn back between the needles and to the back of the work, making sure your bead is lying at the front of the work. The bead is now in a secured position. Continue with the pattern as usual.

WORKING A SIMPLE BEADED SWATCH

Thread 119 beads onto the yarn. Cast on 35 stitches.
Row 1: Knit.
Row 2: Purl.
Repeat rows 1–2 once more.
Row 5: *Knit 1, bead 1, repeat from * to the last stitch, knit 1.
Repeat rows 2–5, 6 more times. Bind off.

basic color work

Changing color can sound quite intimidating, but actually the most difficult thing about it is keeping your yarns from tangling.

RACHEL'S TIP: There are two different types of color knitting—Fair Isle and intarsia. Whichever method you use, wind as much yarn of each color as possible onto its own bobbin and work from the bobbins. This will help prevent the yarns from tangling up.

Fair Isle is used when a color pattern is being repeated right along a row. The yarn that is not being knitted with at any point in the pattern is woven into the back of the knitted fabric using either the weaving or stranding technique. Therefore, a Fair Isle fabric is effectively double-thickness and can be quite stiff. Be very careful not to pull the woven or stranded yarn too tight, or the fabric will bunch up on the front.

Intarsia knitting is used when you are working a large motif in a knitted fabric. Each section of color (the motif and the background on either side) uses a separate ball of yarn. The yarns need to be looped around each other at the edges of each section to avoid holes.

JOINING YARN

❶ When joining a new shade of yarn into a row of stitches, place the end of the yarn between the tips of the needles and across the main shade from left to right.

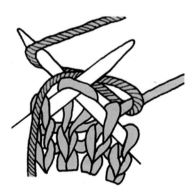

❷ Take the new yarn under the main yarn and knit the next stitch with it. Move the end of the main shade off the needle as the new stitch is formed.

WEAVING IN COLOR

Use this method if more than 4 stitches of the same shade are being worked.

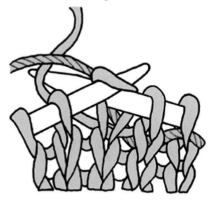

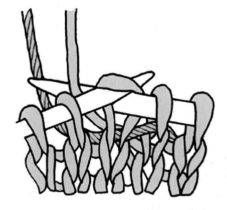

❶ To weave in yarn on the right side (a knit row), insert the right-hand needle into the next stitch and lay the yarn to be woven in over the right-hand needle. Knit the stitch with the main shade of yarn, taking it under the yarn not in use.

❷ Knit the next stitch with the main shade of yarn, taking it over the yarn being woven in. Continue to do this, weaving the yarn not in use over and under the main shade of yarn until you need to start working with it again.

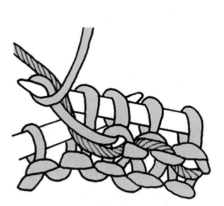

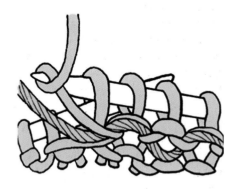

❸ To weave on the wrong side (a purl row), do the same as you would do for the right side, but purl the stitch with the main shade of yarn and take it under the yarn not in use.

❹ Purl the next stitch with the main shade of yarn, taking it over the yarn being woven in. Continue to do this, weaving the yarn not in use over and under the main shade of yarn until you need to start working with it again.

STRANDING COLOR

Use this method if fewer than 4 stitches of the same shade are being worked.

1. On the right side (a knit row), when knitting the first stitch in a group in the main shade of yarn, insert the right-hand needle into the stitch and take the main shade over the contrast shade of yarn. Knit the main shade stitches.

2. When knitting the first stitch in a group in the contrast shade of yarn, insert the right-hand needle into the stitch and take the contrast shade under the main shade. Knit the contrast shade stitches.

3. On the wrong side (a purl row), when purling the first stitch in a group in the main shade, insert the right-hand needle into the next stitch and take the main shade over the contrast shade. Purl the main shade stitches.

4. When purling the first stitch in a group in the contrast shade, insert the right-hand needle into the next stitch and take the contrast shade under the main shade. Purl the contrast shade stitches.

5. Your knitted fabric should look nice and neat on the wrong side, where all the stranded color will be visible (see below).

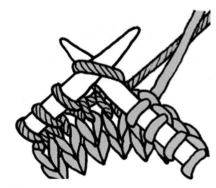

INTARSIA

Use this method to work a larger color motif.

On the right side (a knit row), when knitting the first stitch in a new shade of yarn, insert the right-hand needle into the stitch and take the old shade over the new shade of yarn (see above). Knit all the stitches in the new shade.

On the wrong side (a purl row), when purling the first stitch in a new shade, insert the right-hand needle into the next stitch and again, take the old shade over the new shade. Purl all the stitches in the new shade.

Use these techniques every time you start working with a new shade of yarn. On the back of the knitted fabric the yarns will end up looped around each other along the color joins, preventing unwanted holes appearing between colors.

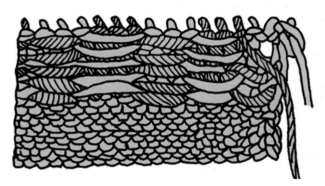

FOLLOWING A CHART/GRAPH

When following a chart, always start with a knit row and the right-hand side of the chart. The arrows on the chart below indicate which direction to go in. So, you start at arrow number 1 and read all the odd-numbered rows from right to left and the even-numbered rows from left to right. Each represents 1 stitch and is colored to match the yarn used.

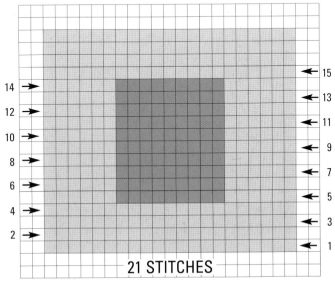

21 STITCHES

cabling

A cable is simply a group of twisted stitches, created by placing a number of stitches on a cable needle and holding them at the front or back of the work.

RACHEL'S TIP: To make them show up well, cables are usually worked in stockinette stitch on a background of reverse stockinette stitch. In these diagrams the stitches being cabled are shown in a darker color so you can see what is happening more clearly.

The cables shown here are worked over 6 stitches, though this number can vary. A back cable worked over 6 stitches is abbreviated as "C6B" and a front cable as "C6F." If they were worked over 4 stitches they would be "C4B" and "C4F." A front cable makes the stitches twist to the left and a back cable makes them twist to the right.

CABLING TO THE FRONT

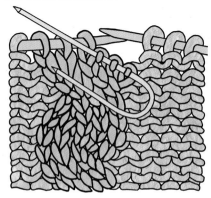

1 Knit to the position of the cable. Using a cable needle, pick up the next 3 stitches, holding the cable needle at the front of the work.

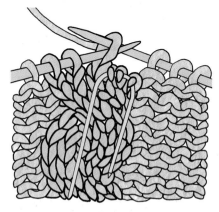

2 Now, knit the next 3 stitches on the left-hand needle, ignoring the stitches on the cable needle.

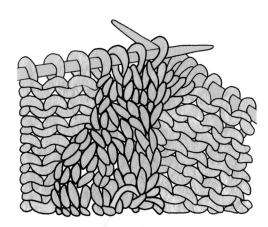

③ Slip the 3 stitches on the cable needle onto the left-hand needle and knit them.

CABLING TO THE BACK

Do the same as above, but hold the cable needle at the back of the work. You can knit the stitches straight from the cable needle if it's easier.

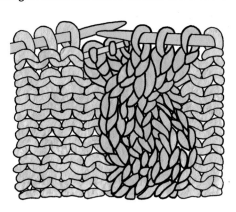

WORKING A SIMPLE CABLE SWATCH

This is an example of a basic cable pattern and it has been worked over 6 rows.

Cast on 42 stitches.
Row 1: p4, k6, p8, k6, p8, k6, p4.
Row 2: k4, p6, k8, p6, k8, p6, k4.
Row 3: As row 1.
Row 4: As row 2.
Row 5: p4, C6F, p8, C6F, p8, C6F, p4.
Row 6: As row 2.

Repeat these 6 rows 3 more times.
Bind off.

pom-poms

I love making pom-poms and I make them in many different sizes and yarns, even combining yarns in one pom-pom—perfect for when you need a break from knitting.

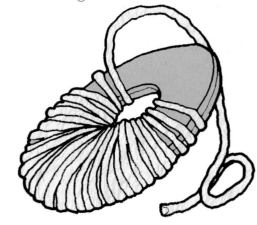

1 Cut two pieces of cardboard of the same diameter and cut a small round hole in the middle of each circle. Place them together and wind your yarn through the holes in the middle of the two pieces of cardboard and around the outer circles.

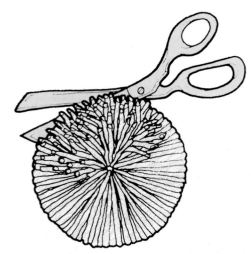

2 Repeat until you have the required amount of yarn wound around both circles. Then, using a pair of scissors, cut the yarn between both circles of cardboard so that the loops are cut open.

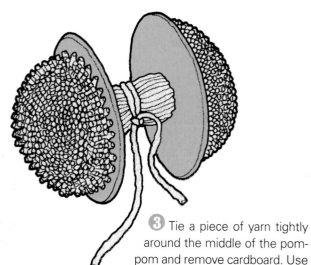

3 Tie a piece of yarn tightly around the middle of the pom-pom and remove cardboard. Use the yarn to attach the pom-pom.

felting

Felting is a really fun technique that will hide any flaws in your knitting, as well as creating a funky decorative finish.

Felting occurs when a woolen item is washed at a hot temperature in the washing machine. This results in the item shrinking and becoming thicker. The fibers bind together to make felted wool, which you can then cut into as it won't fray or unravel. This is because as the washing machine tumbles the knitting around, the agitation causes the wool to rub together and "knit" itself tighter.

This is a great technique for beginners as any flaws or holes in the knitting tend to close up and disappear because of the shrinkage. It is also great if you don't want to spend a lot of time knitting a project or if you want to be a little bit more experimental.

The types of yarn that are most suitable for felting are those made of 100 percent wool. The more wool your yarn contains and the higher the temperature, the better your knitted fabric will felt.

TO FELT

Just put the knitted pieces into the machine and wash them at a hot temperature. It's that easy! I always put mine in a pillowcase as it helps agitate the fabric and help the felting. Or you could throw in an old pair of jeans or a towel. Once you have felted your knitting and left it to dry thoroughly, you can cut out your required pattern.

abbreviations

Although knitting patterns can look like a jumble of letters, you will soon become familiar with these abbreviations.

approx	Approximately
beg	Beginning
C6B	Cable 6 back
C6F	Cable 6 front
cont	Continue
DK	Double knitting
dec	Decrease
inc	Increase
k	Knit
k2tog	Knit two stitches together
k2tbl	Knit two stitches together by going through the back of both stitches.
MB	Make bobble
M1	Make a stitch
p	Purl
psso	Pass slipped stitch over
RS	Right side
Sl 1	Slip 1 stitch
sl 1, k1, skpo	Slip 1 stitch, knit 1 stitch, pass slipped stitch over
st (s)	Stitch(es)
st st	Stockinette stitch
tbl	Through back of loop(s)
turn	Swap needles so work faces the opposite way
WS	Wrong side
YF	Yarn forward
YO	Yarn over
YRN	Yarn round needle

KNITTING TERMS

Asterisks and square brackets

These are used to show where a piece of work is to be repeated. For example if a pattern says to k1, *p1, k1* 3 times, you will repeat the p1, k1 in between the asterisks 3 times in total. Similarly, you repeat instructions within square brackets the stated number of times.

Stitches at the end of a row

Sometimes in a pattern, you will see a number of stitches shown in brackets, e.g. (16 stitches) at the end of a row. This is a useful marker so you can check that you have the right number of stitches on your needle.

Charts and graphs

These are used to show color pattern instead of written instructions. Each square on the graph resembles a stitch (see page 37).

Flower Corsage (p48)

Bow-tie Necklace
(p74)

Record Bag (p77)

Silk Evening Scarf
(p66)

Guy's Scarf (p73),
Girl's Casual Scarf (p47)

accessories for guys & girls

To get you started, here are some projects that you can knit for yourself—scarves, bags, and some beaded jewelry.

girl's casual scarf

I designed this piece on the train to Fife to visit my parents, huddled up in the corner of the car with my cable pin and some chunky wool. Cabling is a great way to be experimental with knitting and it's so easy to do.

MATERIALS 4 x 100g balls of Rowan Big Wool Fusion.

NEEDLES 1 pair of US 19 (15mm) needles. Cable needle.

GAUGE 7 stitches and 10 rows to 4in/10cm square over stockinette stitch.

ABBREVIATIONS

Cable 6 front: Slip next 3 stitches onto a cable needle and hold at front of work, knit 3 stitches from left-hand needle, then knit 3 from cable needle.

Cable 6 back: Slip next 3 stitches onto a cable needle and hold at back of work, knit 3 stitches from left-hand needle, then knit 3 from cable needle (see page 38).

PATTERN

Cast on 28 stitches.
Row 1: Knit to end of row.
Row 2: Purl to end of row.
Row 3: Knit 2, [cable 6 front, knit 2] twice, cable 6 front, knit 4 .
Row 4: Purl to end of row.
Row 5: Knit 4, [cable 6 back, knit 2] twice, cable 6 back, knit 2.
Repeat rows 2–5 until 3 balls have been knitted. Bind off.

TO MAKE UP

Use fourth ball of yarn to make a fringe for the ends of the scarf. Cut 14in/36cm lengths of yarn and loop them through the cast on and bound off stitches.

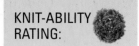

flower corsage

I love knitting flowers and I started knitting this one on a bus ride to Aberdeen to visit friends and then finished it on the way back. This would look lovely pinned on to a suit jacket or even as an accessory for a purse.

MATERIALS 1 x 50g ball of RYC Soft Tweed in each of two shades A and B. Elastic thread.

NEEDLES 1 pair of US 10 (6mm) needles.

GAUGE 12 stitches and 16 rows to 10cm/4in square over stockinette stitch

ABBREVIATIONS

M1: Make 1 stitch by picking up the strand between the stitch on the right-hand needle and the stitch on the left-hand needle and placing it on the left-hand needle, then knit into the back of it (see page 26).

K2tbl: Knit the next 2 stitches together by going through the back of both stitches.

PATTERN

Main part
Using A, cast on 8 stitches.
Row 1: Knit to end of row.
Row 2: Knit to end of row.
Row 3: Knit 1, M1 and knit to end of row.
Row 4: Knit to end of row.
Row 5: Knit 1, M1 and knit to end of row.
Rows 6, 7 and 8: Knit to end to row.
Row 9: K2tbl, knit to end of row.
Row 10: Knit to end of row.
Row 11: As row 9.
Row 12: Knit to end of row.
Row 13: Bind off 4 stitches, knit to end of row. (4 stitches).
Row 14: Knit to end of row.
Row 15: Cast on 4 stitches, knit to end of row.
Repeat rows 2–15, 9 more times, then repeat rows 2–14 again.
Bind off.

Middle of flower

Using B, cast on 5 stitches.

Row 1: Knit to end of row.

Row 2: Purl to end of row.

Row 3: Knit 1, M1, knit 3, M1, knit 1. (7 stitches).

Row 4: Purl to end of row.

Row 5: Knit 2 stitches together, knit 3, knit 2 stitches together. (5 stitches).

Row 6: Purl to end of row.

Row 7: Knit to end of row.

Row 8: Knit 2 stitches together.

Bind off.

TO MAKE UP

Pass the elastic thread through the straight edge of the main part, then pull tightly to form a rosette shape. Sew the middle into the center of corsage.

#1 EXTREME KNITTING

Knitting at the top of Arthur's Seat, Edinburgh, Scotland

THINGS TO DO WITH YOUR KNITTING NEEDLES:

#1 USE THEM AS COCKTAIL STIRRERS

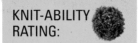

muff

Knit this simple design to look cool among your friends and keep your fingers nice 'n' cozy in the freezing winter weather.

MATERIALS 1 x 100g ball of Rowan Big Wool in each of 2 shades A and B.

NEEDLES 1 pair of US 15 (10mm) needles.

GAUGE 10 stitches and 13 rows to 4in/10cm square over stockinette stitch.

ABBREVIATIONS

Loop 1 (a loop stitch): Knit the next stitch, but do not take stitch off left-hand needle, take the yarn forward between the needles, pass yarn around left thumb and then to back of work between the needles, knit into the same stitch again and remove from left-hand needle. Wind yarn over right-hand needle once, then pass the 2 stitches over this stitch, knit next stitch.

Note: Carry yarn that is not in use up the side of the work; twist yarns neatly on every alternate row.

PATTERN

Using A, cast on 23 stitches.
Row 1: Knit to end of row.
Row 2: Purl to end of row.
Row 3: Knit 1, *Loop 1, knit 1*, repeat from * to end of row.
Row 4: Purl to end.
Rows 5–24: Repeat rows 1–4, 5 more times.
Rows 25–28: Using B, purl to end of row.
Rows 29–32: Using A, purl to end of row.
Rows 33–36: Using B, purl to end of row.
Rows 37–40: Using A, purl to end of row.
Using A, bind off.

TO MAKE UP

Sew up using mattress stitch (see page 31) by joining cast on and bound off edge together. Make strap by braiding 3 strands of B together. Sew ends to edge of seam.

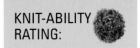
stripey hat & gloves

Loud, bright, and very warm, I designed this matching set to cheer myself up over winter and then to top them off, I added bows to the fingerless gloves. I love bows because I always think they look great as a feature on a knitted design, and they are really simple to make.

For the hat

MATERIALS 1 x 100g ball of Rowan Big Wool in each of two shades A and B.

NEEDLES 1 pair of US 15 (10mm) needles.

GAUGE 10 stitches and 13 rows to 4in/10cm square over stockinette stitch.

Note: Carry yarn that is not in use up the side of the work, twist yarns neatly on every alternate row.

PATTERN

Using A, cast on 40 stitches.
Row 1: Knit 1, *purl 2, knit 2, repeat from* to last 3 stitches, purl 2, knit 1.
Row 2: Purl 1, *knit 2, purl 2, repeat from * to last 3 stitches, knit 2, purl 1.
Rows 3–6: Repeat rows 1–2 twice more.

Row 7: Using B, knit to end of row.
Row 8: Using B, purl to end of row.
Row 9: Using A, knit to end of row.
Row 10: Using A, purl to end of row.
Rows 11–16: Repeat rows 7–10 once more, then rows 7–8.
Row 17: Using A, [knit 7, knit 3 stitches together] 4 times.
Row 18: Using A, purl to end of row.
Row 19: Using B, [knit 5, knit 3 stitches together] 4 times.
Row 20: Using B, purl to end of row.
Row 21: Using A, [knit 3, knit 3 stitches together] 4 times.
Row 22: Using A, [purl 2 stitches together] 8 times. Bind off.

Break yarn and thread through remaining stitches. Pull up tight and fasten off securely.

TO MAKE UP

Join seam using mattress stitch (see page 31).

For the gloves

MATERIALS 1 x 100g ball of Rowan Big Wool in each of two shades A and B.

NEEDLES 1 pair of US 15 (10mm) needles.

GAUGE 10 stitches and 13 rows to 4in/ 10cm square over stockinette stitch.

ABBREVIATIONS

Turn: Swap needles, so work faces the other way.

PATTERN

Left hand
Using A, cast on 20 stitches.
Row 1: Knit 1, *purl 2, knit 2, repeat from * to last 3 stitches, purl 2, knit 1.
Row 2: Purl 1, *knit 2, purl 2, repeat from * to last 3 stitches, knit 2, purl 1.
Rows 3–6: Repeat rows 1 and 2 twice more.
Row 7: Using A, knit to end of row.
Row 8: Using A, purl to end.
Row 9: Using B, knit to end.
Row 10: Using B, purl to end of row.
Rows 11–14: Repeat rows 7–10.
Rows 15–16: Repeat rows 7–8.
Row 17 (make bow): Using B, knit 12, turn, cast on 12 stitches, turn, knit to end of row. (32 stitches).
Row 18: Using B, purl to end.
Rows 19–20: Repeat rows 7–8.
Row 21 (make thumb hole): Using B, knit 4, bring yarn forward and over needle, knit 2 stitches together, knit to end.

Row 22: Using B, purl to end of row.
Row 23: Using A, knit 12, bind off 12, knit to end.
Row 24: Using A, purl to end of row.
Rows 25–26: Repeat rows 9–10.
Bind off.

Right hand
Using A, cast on 20 stitches.
Row 1: Knit 1, *purl 2, knit 2, repeat from * to last 3 stitches, knit 1.
Row 2: Purl 1, *knit 2, purl 2, repeat from * to last 3 stitches, knit 2, purl 1.
Rows 3–6: Repeat rows 1–2 twice more.
Row 7: Using A, knit to end of row.
Row 8: Using A, purl to end of row.
Row 9: Using B, knit to end of row.
Row 10: Using B, purl to end of row.
Rows 11–14: Repeat rows 7–10.
Rows 15–16: Repeat rows 7–8.
Row 17 (make bow): Using B, knit 8, turn, cast on 12 stitches, turn, knit to end of row. (32 stitches).
Row 18: Using B, purl to end of row.
Rows 19 to 20: Repeat rows 7–8.
Row 21 (make thumbhole): Using B, knit 14, knit 2 stitches together. Bring yarn forward and over needle, knit to end of row.
Row 22: Using B, purl to end.
Row 23: Using A, knit 12, bind off 12, knit to end.
Row 24: Using A, purl to end.
Rows 25–26: Repeat rows 9–10.
Bind off.

TO MAKE UP

Sew sides together using mattress stitch (see page 31). Using A, sew up the gap underneath the bow from the inside, carry yarn around center of bow and pull tight to create bow shape.

THINGS TO DO WITH YOUR WOOL: #1 **USE IT AS A CLOTHESLINE**

small purse

I love using Ribbon Twist, it's one of my favorite yarns and always looks good when knitted up. This mini purse would be great for taking on a night out, a perfect size for your money, phone, and makeup.

MATERIALS 2 x 100g balls of Rowan Ribbon Twist.
4 Rowan buttons.

NEEDLES 1 pair of US 17 (12mm) needles.
Cable needle.

GAUGE 9 stitches and 13 rows to 4in/10cm square over stockinette stitch.

ABBREVIATIONS

Cable 10 back: Slip the next 5 stitches onto a cable needle and hold at back of work, knit 5 stitches from left-hand needle, then knit 5 from cable needle (see page 38).

Yarn forward: Bring yarn forward between the needles, then take it over the right-hand needle to make 1 stitch.

PATTERN

Main part
Cast on 28 stitches.
Row 1: Knit to end of row.
Row 2: Purl to end of row.
Row 3: Knit to end of row.
Row 4: Purl to end of row.
Row 5: Knit 2, cable 10 back, knit 4, cable 10 back, knit 2.
Row 6: Purl to end of row.
Rows 7–38: Repeat rows 1–6, 5 more times, then rows 1 and 2 again.
Bind off.

Gusset (make 2)
Cast on 5 stitches.
Row 1: Knit to end of row.
Row 2: Purl to end of row.
Rows 3–18: Repeat rows 1–2, 8 more times.
Bind off.

Handles (make 2)

Cast on 6 stitches.

Row 1: Knit to end of row.

Row 2: Purl to end of row.

Row 3 (buttonhole row): Knit 3, yarn forward, knit 2 together, knit 1.

Row 4: Purl to end of row.

Rows 5 to 42: Repeat rows 1–2, 19 more times.

Row 43 (buttonhole row): Knit 3, yarn forward, knit 2 together, knit 1.

Row 44: Purl to end of row.

Rows 45–46: As rows 1–2.

Bind off.

TO MAKE UP

With center of cast on edge of gussets to center of side of main part, sew gussets in place using mattress stitch (see page 31). Sew on buttons to bag. Button handles in place.

THINGS TO DO WITH YOUR KNITTING NEEDLES:

#2 USE THEM TO LABEL YOUR HOUSEPLANTS!

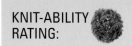

two-color scarf

This was one of the first designs I did for this book. It looks more difficult to do than it actually is and is just a matter of increasing and decreasing. I began it at my first knitting circle and the following week it was complete!

MATERIALS   1 x 50g ball of Rowan Kid Classic in each of 2 shades A and B.

NEEDLES   1 pair of US 9 (5.5mm) needles.

GAUGE   18 stitches and 23 rows to 4in/10cm square over stockinette stitch.

ABBREVIATIONS

Turn: Swap needles, so work faces the other way.

Note: Carry yarn not in use up the side of the work; twist yarns neatly on every alternate row.

PATTERN

Using A, cast on 18 stitches.

Rows 1–6: Knit to end of row.
Row 7: Bind off 14 stitches, knit to end of row.
Row 8: Change to B, knit 4, turn and cast on 14 stitches.
Rows 9–14: Knit to end of row.
Row 15: Bind off 14 stitches, knit to end of row.
Row 16: Change to A, knit 4, turn and cast on 14 stitches.
Repeat rows 1–16, 25 more times.
Repeat rows 1–6.
Bind off all stitches.

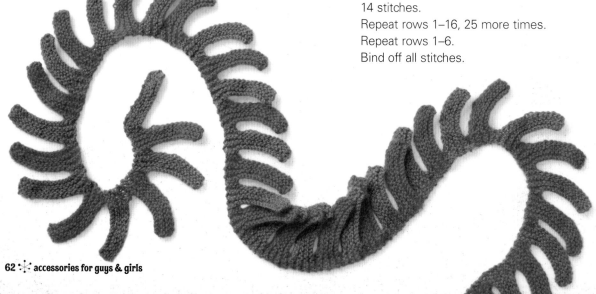

fluffy shawl

I created this on Christmas day with festive spirit. The brushed wool looks enchanting and you could wear this to a party or to keep cozy in the evening.

MATERIALS 5 x 100g balls of Rowan Biggy Print. 60in/1.5m ribbon.

NEEDLES 1 pair of US 15 (10mm) needles.

GAUGE 9 stitches and 11 rows to 4in/10cm square over stockinette stitch.

ABBREVIATIONS

Loop 1 (a loop stitch): Knit the next stitch, but do not take stitch off left-hand needle, yarn forward between the needles, pass yarn around left thumb and then to back of work between the needles, knit into the same stitch again and remove from needle. Wind yarn over needle once, then pass the 2 stitches over this stitch.

PATTERN

(Make 2 pieces)

Cast on 20 stitches.

Row 1: Purl 1, *knit 1, purl 1, repeat from * to last stitch, knit 1.
Row 2: Knit 1, *purl 1, knit 1, repeat from * to last stitch, purl 1.
Row 3: Purl 1, *knit 1, purl 1, repeat from * to last stitch, knit 1.
Row 4: Knit 1, *purl 1, knit 1, repeat from * to last stitch, purl 1.
Row 5: Purl 1, * loop 1, repeat from * to last stitch, knit 1.
Row 6: Knit 1, *purl 1, knit 1, repeat from * to last stitch, purl 1.
Rows 7–30: Repeat rows 1–6, 4 more times.
Bind off.

TO MAKE UP

Join the two panels together using back stitch or mattress stitch. Cut each loop and tie in a knot, brush out each strand to create brushed out fluffy effect. Cut ribbon in half and sew one piece to each front.

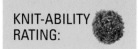
silk evening scarf

Kidsilk Haze is a really delicate yarn, so I designed a scarf you could wear as an everyday accessory or on a night out. You will need to use double thickness here, so wind the yarn into two equal-sized balls before you begin.

MATERIALS 1 x 25g ball of Rowan Kidsilk Haze Night. Wind into 2 balls.

NEEDLES 1 pair of US 8 (5mm) needles.

GAUGE 25 stitches and 34 rows to 4in/10cm square over stockinette stitch.

ABBREVIATIONS

M1: Make 1 stitch by picking up the strand between the stitch on the right-hand needle and the stitch on the left-hand needle and placing it on the left-hand needle, then knit into the back of it (see page 26).

PATTERN

Cast on 8 stitches.
Row 1: Knit to end of row.
Row 2: Knit to end of row.
Row 3: Knit 1, M1, knit to end of row.
Row 4: Knit to end of row.
Row 5: Knit 1, M1, knit to end of row.
Rows 6, 7 and 8: Knit to end of row.
Row 9: Knit 2 together through the back of the stitches, knit to end of row.
Row 10: Knit to end of row.
Row 11: Knit 2 together through the back of the stitches, knit to end of row.
Row 12: Knit to end of row.
Row 13: Bind off 4 stitches, knit to end of row.
Row 14: Knit 4.
Row 15: Cast on 4 stitches, knit these 4 stitches, knit to end.
Repeat rows 2–15 until there is enough yarn left to bind off, ending with a row 13. Bind off.

bumpy bag

I'm forever losing my wool and needles around my apartment. This bag is the perfect solution and will keep all your knitting stuff together—just pick it up and take it traveling, to a café or to your knitting circle.

MATERIALS

4 x 100g balls of Rowan Biggy Print. 1 x 100g ball of Rowan Spray—wind into 2 balls.

NEEDLES

1 pair of US 19 (15mm) needles.

GAUGE

7 stitches and 10 rows to 4in/10cm square over stockinette stitch.

ABBREVIATIONS

MB (make bobble): (knit 1, purl 1, knit 1, purl 1, knit 1) all into next stitch, turn needles and purl 5 stitches, turn needles and knit 5 stitches, turn needles and purl 2 stitches together, purl 1, purl 2 stitches together, turn needles, knit 3 stitches together.

Turn: Swap needles, so work faces the other way.

PATTERN

(Make 2 pieces)
Using Biggy Print, cast on 11 stitches.

Row 1: Knit to end of row.
Row 2: Purl to end of row.
Row 3: Knit 1, *MB, knit 1, repeat from * to end.
Row 4: Purl to end of row.
Rows 5–10: Repeat rows 1–2, 3 more times.

Repeat rows 1–10, 2 more times.
Break off Biggy Print.

Join in 2 ends of Spray and use double thickness.

Next row: Knit 1, [purl 2, knit 2] twice, purl 2.
Next row: Knit 2, [purl 2, knit 2] twice, purl 1.
Repeat the last 2 rows once more.
Bind off.

Gusset (make 2)
Using Biggy Print, cast on 5 stitches.

Row 1: Knit to end of row.
Row 2: Purl to end of row.
Repeat these 2 rows until gusset fits from center of cast on edge of main part to beginning of rib section of back and front, ending with a row 2. Break off Biggy Print.

Join on two ends of Spray and use double thickness.

Next row: Knit 1, purl 2, knit 2.
Next row: Purl 2, knit 2, purl 1.

Repeat the last 2 rows once more.
Bind off.

Handle (make 2)
Using two ends of Spray, cast on 6 stitches.

Row 1: Knit 1, purl 2, knit 2, purl 1.
Rows 2–18: Repeat row 1, 17 times.
Bind off.

TO MAKE UP

Join cast on edges of gusset pieces. With gusset seam to center of cast on edge of main part sew gussets in place. Sew on handles.

THINGS TO DO WITH YOUR KNITTING NEEDLES: #3 USE THEM AS CHOPSTICKS!

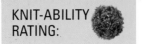
guy's chunky scarf

I designed this in order to inspire a guy to knit it, but it would be a great scarf for a girl as well. The diagonal stripes make it look harder than it is, but the technique is really simple and it will just take you an evening to do.

MATERIALS
2 x 100g balls of Rowan Biggy Print in each of 2 shades A and B.

NEEDLES
1 pair of US 36 (20mm) needles.

GAUGE
7 stitches and 10 rows over 4in/ 10cm square over stockinette stitch.

Note: Carry yarn not in use up the side of the work; twist yarns neatly on every alternate row.

ABBREVIATIONS

M1: Make 1 stitch by picking up the strand between the stitch on the right-hand needle and the stitch on the left-hand needle and placing it on the left-hand needle, then knit into the back of it (see page 26).

PATTERN

Using A, cast on 12 stitches.
Row 1: Knit 2 together, knit to end of row.
Row 2: Knit 1, M1, knit to end of row.
Row 3: Knit 2 together, knit to end of row.
Row 4: Knit 1, M1, knit to end of row.

Change to B.
Rows 5–8: Using B, work as rows 1–4.
Repeat rows 1–8, 8 more times.
Using B bind off.

bow-tie necklace

I designed this while spending time with some friends on a lazy Friday evening. As I beaded away, my friends caught up with one another, and before I knew it, my necklace was complete!

MATERIAL   1 x 50g ball of Rowan Kid Classic. 3 packets of Jaeger beads (about 400 beads).

NEEDLES   1 pair of US 9 (5.5mm) needles.

GAUGE   18 stitches and 23 rows to 4in/10cm square over stockinette stitch.

ABBREVIATIONS

Bead 1 (B1): Bring yarn to front of work between the needles, slide 1 bead up close to work, slip next stitch, take yarn to back of work (see page 32).

PATTERN

Thread on 297 of your chosen beads before casting on.
Each bead row requires 9 beads.

Cast on 19 stitches.
Row 1: Knit to end of row.
Row 2: Knit 1, purl to last stitch, knit 1.
Row 3: Knit 1, *bead 1, knit 1, repeat from * to end.
Row 4: Knit 1, purl to last stitch, knit 1.
Row 5: Knit to end of row.
Row 6: Knit 1, purl to last stitch, knit 1.
Repeat rows 1–6, 32 more times.
Bind off.

TO MAKE UP

Press the knitted fabric. Tie the long piece of beaded fabric into a bow, securing with some Kid Classic.

Make a chain by threading 100 beads onto a length of Kid Classic and sew each end to the top of the bow (see photograph).

record bag

My brother came up with this idea, as he wanted a bag he could carry around. You can use it to carry records, or your change purse or wallet, and phone. When working from the chart, use the intarsia method (see page 36).

MATERIALS 3 x 50g balls of Rowan Handknit Cotton DK in main color (M). 1 x ball in contrast color (C). 12in/30cm zipper.

NEEDLES 1 pair of US 6 (4mm) needles.

GAUGE 20 stitches and 28 rows to 4in/ 10cm square over stockinette stitch.

PATTERN

Back and front (make 2)
Using M, cast on 8 stitches.
Work circle in stockinette stitch, following the chart on the following page, shaping sides by increasing, casting on, decreasing or binding off, as required (see overleaf). Bind off.

Handle
Cast on 16 stitches.
Continue in stockinette stitch until handle measures 60ins/150cm.
Bind off.

Zipper placket (make 2)
Cast on 10 stitches.
Continue in stockinette stitch until placket measures 20ins/50cm.
Bind off.

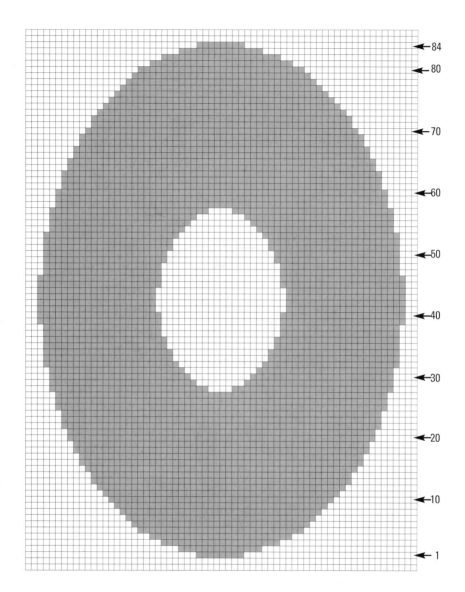

← 84
← 80
← 70
← 60
← 50
← 40
← 30
← 20
← 10
← 1

TO MAKE UP

Using mattress stitch, join placket pieces together for 6in/15cm at each end, leaving 12in/30cm open at center. Sew in zipper. Join cast on and bound off edges of handle together. Leaving 20in/50cm free, sew handle between back and front to form gusset join at center of cast on edges. Sew zipper placket in place, tucking ends in behind handle.

CHART

See page 37 for instructions for following a chart.

To increase a single stitch, use Inc1 (see page 27) on the edges of the knitting. To increase several stitches, cast them on. To decrease a single stitch, use k2tog or p2tog (see page 28). To decrease several stitches, bind them off.

Glasses Case (p100)

Slippers (p82)

Laptop Case (p87)

Coasters (p96)

Tea Cosy (p91)

knitting for an occasion

Once you have gained more confidence, you can make gifts for your friends—something that you can style to suit their tastes and personality.

slippers

Last Christmas I bought my roommate a pair of red chunky slippers, this year I thought I'd knit her a pair instead. They are really easy to do as I've just used stockinette stitch, and they are really quick to knit up.

MATERIALS
4 x 100g balls of Rowan Biggy Print.

NEEDLES
1 pair of US 19 (15mm) needles.

GAUGE
7 stitches and 10 rows to 4in/10cm square over stockinette stitch.

ABBREVIATIONS

M1: Make 1 stitch by picking up the strand between the stitch on the right-hand needle and the stitch on the left-hand needle and placing it on the left-hand needle, then knit into the back of it (see page 26).

PATTERN

Front (make 2)
Cast on 9 stitches.

Row 1: Knit to end of row.
Row 2: Purl to end of row.
Row 3: Slip 1, knit 1, pass slipped stitch over stitch just knitted, knit 5, knit 2 stitches together.
Row 4: Purl to end of row.
Row 5: Slip 1, knit 1, pass slipped stitch over stitch just knitted, knit 3, knit 2 stitches together.
Row 6: Purl to end of row.
Row 7: Slip 1, knit 1, pass slipped stitch over stitch just knitted, knit 1, knit 2 stitches together.
Row 8: Purl 3 together and fasten off.

Left side (make 2)
Cast on 13 stitches.

Row 1: Knit to end of row.
Row 2: Purl to end of row.
Row 3: Knit 1, M1, knit to end of row. (14 stitches).
Row 4: Purl to end of row.
Row 5: Knit 1, M1, knit to end of row. (15 stitches).
Row 6: Purl to end of row.
Row 7: Knit 1, M1, knit to end of row. (16 stitches).
Row 8: Purl to end of row.
Row 9: [Slip 1, knit 1, pass slipped stitch over stitch just knitted] twice, knit to end of row. (14 stitches).
Row 10: Purl to end of row.
Row 11: [Slip 1, knit 1, pass slipped stitch over stitch just knitted] twice, knit to end. (12 stitches).
Row 12: Purl to end of row.
Row 13: [Slip 1, knit 1, pass slipped stitch over stitch just knitted] twice, knit to end. (10 stitches).
Row 14: Purl to end of row.
Row 15: [Slip 1, knit 1, pass slipped stitch over stitch just knitted] twice, knit to end. (8 stitches). Bind off.

Right side (make 2)

Cast on 13 stitches.
Row 1: Knit to end of row.
Row 2: Purl to end of row.
Row 3: Knit to last stitch, M1, k1. (14 stitches).
Row 4: Purl to end of row.
Row 5: Knit to last stitch, M1, k1. (15 stitches).
Row 6: Purl to end of row.
Row 7: Knit to last stitch, M1, k1. (16 stitches).
Row 8: Purl to end of row.
Row 9: Knit to last 4 stitches, [knit 2 stitches together] twice. (14 stitches).
Row 10: Purl to end of row.
Row 11: Knit to last 4 stitches, [knit 2 stitches together] twice. (12 stitches).
Row 12: Purl to end of row.
Row 13: Knit to last 4 stitches, [knit 2 stitches together] twice. (10 stitches).
Row 14: Purl to end of row.
Row 15: Knit to last 4 stitches, [knit 2 stitches together] twice. (8 stitches).
Bind off.

Sole (make 2)

Cast on 5 stitches.
Row 1: Knit to end of row.
Row 2: Purl to end of row.
Row 3: Knit 1, M1, knit to last stitch, M1, knit 1 (7 stitches).
Row 4: Purl to end of row.
Row 5: Knit 1, M1, knit to last stitch, M1, knit 1 (9 stitches).
Row 6: Purl to end of row.
Rows 7 to 14: Work in stockinette stitch.
Row 15: Slip 1, knit 1, pass slipped stitch over stitch just knitted, knit to last 2 stitches, knit 2 stitches together. (7 stitches).
Row 16: Purl to end of row.
Row 17: Slip 1, knit 1, pass slipped stitch over stitch just knitted, knit to last 2 stitches, knit 2 stitches together. (5 stitches).

Row 18: Purl to end of row.
Bind off.

TO MAKE UP

Sew up using mattress stitch (see page 31), but instead of working on the right sides, work on the wrong sides to create a visible seam. Join left and right side from cast off edge to "point." Then sew row ends of front to remaining row ends of left and right sides, then join to sole.

POM-POMS

Use two 2in/5cm diameter circles of cardboard and the remaining yarn to make two pom-poms (see page 40). Attach to slippers by darning in the binding yarn around the ankle of the slipper, so that you can pull to tighten slipper.

#3 EXTREME KNITTING

Lovely ladies knitting in Nigeria.

laptop case

Even a laptop needs some beauty sleep in the hustle and bustle of everyday life, so wrap it up in this bobbly cover and give it the rest it deserves—a perfect graduation gift.

MATERIALS 1 x 100g ball of Rowan Biggy Print in Shade A.
2 x balls in Shade B.
4 x buttons.

NEEDLES 1 pair of US 17 (12mm) needles.

GAUGE 8 stitches and 11 rows to 4in/10cm square over stockinette stitch.

ABBREVIATIONS

MB (make bobble): (knit 1, purl 1, knit 1, purl 1, knit 1) all into next stitch, turn needles and purl 5 stitches, turn needles and knit 5 stitches, turn needles and purl 2 stitches together, purl 1, purl 2 stitches together, turn needles, knit 3 stitches together.

Turn: Swap needles, so work faces the other way.

YO (yarn over): take yarn over the needle to make 1 stitch.

Note: Carry yarn that is not in use up the side of the work; twist yarns neatly on every alternate row.

PATTERN

Main piece
Using B, cast on 20 stitches.

Row 1: Knit 1, *purl 2, knit 2, repeat from * to last 3 stitches, purl 2, knit 1.
Row 2: Purl 1, *knit 2, purl 2, repeat from * to last 3 stitches, knit 2, purl 1.
Row 3: Knit 1, [purl 2, YO, knit 2 stitches together] 4 times, purl 2, knit 1.
Row 4: Purl 1, *knit 2, purl 2, repeat from * to last 3 stitches, knit 2, purl 1.
Row 5: Knit 1, *purl 2, knit 2, repeat from * to last 3 stitches, purl 2, knit 1.
Row 6: Purl 1, *knit 2, purl 2, repeat from * to last 3 stitches, knit 2, purl 1.

Change to A.
Row 7: Knit to end of row.
Row 8: Purl to end of row.
(These 2 rows form stockinette stitch.)

Rows 9–40: Work in stockinette stitch.
Row 41: *Knit 4, MB, repeat from * to last 5 stitches, knit to end of row.

Row 42: Purl to end of row.

Row 43: Knit to end of row.

Row 44: Purl to end of row.

Row 45: Knit 2, *MB, knit 4, repeat from * to last 5 stitches, MB, knit 2.

Row 46: Purl to end of row.

Row 47: Knit to end of row.

Row 48: Purl to end of row.

Rows 49–56: Repeat rows 41–48 once more.

Rows 57–60: Repeat rows 41–44 once more.

Rows 61–62: Using B, work in stockinette stitch.

Rows 63–64: Using A, work in stockinette stitch.

Rows 65–66: Using B, work in stockinette stitch.

Rows 67–70: Using A, work in stockinette stitch.

Rows 71–74: Using B, work in stockinette stitch.

Rows 75–76: Using A, work in stockinette stitch.

Bind off.

Gussets (make 2)

Using A, cast on 4 stitches.

Row 1: Knit to end of row.

Row 2: Purl to end of row.

(These 2 rows form stockinette stitch.)

Rows 3–32: Work in stockinette stitch.

Bind off.

TO MAKE UP

Sew buttons onto row 72. Using mattress stitch, (see page 31), sew gussets to each side of cover, between bound off edge and start of stockinette stitch. Fold over rib part and fasten to buttons.

THINGS TO DO WITH YOUR WOOL:

#3 MAKE A CAT'S CRADLE

tea cosy

I originally saw this idea in a knitting catalog from the 1940s and wanted to come up with my own design that was a bit more modern. A perfect gift for your mom on Mother's Day!

<u>MATERIALS</u>   1 x 50g ball of Rowan Calmer in each of two shades A and B.

<u>NEEDLES</u>   1 pair of US 8 (5mm) needles.

<u>GAUGE</u>   21 stitches and 30 rows to 4in/10cm square over stockinette stitch.

Note: When carrying yarn across back of stitches pull slightly tight to form "pucker" and twist each shade after every 4th stitch. Always twist both yarns at the beginning of the row.

PATTERN

Make 2 pieces.

Using A, cast on 80 stitches.
Row 1: *Using A, knit 10, using B, knit 10, repeat from * to end of row.
Row 2: *Using B, purl 10, using A, purl 10, repeat from * to end of row.

Rows 3–10: Repeat rows 1–2, 4 times.
Row 11: *Using B, knit 10, using A, knit 10, repeat from * to end of row.
Row 12: *Using A, purl 10, using B, purl 10, repeat from * to end of row.
Rows 13–20: Repeat rows 11–12, 4 times.
Rows 21–30: Repeat rows 1–2, 5 times.
Rows 31–36: Repeat rows 11–12, 3 times.
Row 37: *Using B, knit 1, knit 2 stitches together through the back of the stitches, knit 5, knit 2 stitches together. Using A, k1, knit 2 stitches together through the back of the stitches, knit 5, knit 2 together, repeat from * to end of row. (64 stitches).
Row 38: * Using A, purl 1, purl 2 stitches together through the back of the stitches, purl 3, purl 2 stitches together, using B, purl 1, purl 2 stitches together through the back of the stitches, purl 3, purl 2 together, repeat from * to end of row. (48 stitches).
Row 39: * Using B, knit 1, knit 2 stitches together through the back of the stitches, knit 1,

knit 2 stitches together. Using A, knit 1, knit 2 stitches together through the back of the stitches, knit 1, knit 2 stitches together, repeat from * to end of row of row. (32 stitches).

Row 40: *Using A, [purl 2 stitches together] twice, using B [purl 2 stitches together] twice, repeat from * to end of row. (16 stitches).

Bind off.

TO MAKE UP

Join side seams together using mattress stitch, leaving holes for spout and handle. Run a gathering thread through bound off edge and pull up tightly. Secure ends.

POM-POM

Using A, make a large pom-pom (see page 40), and attach to top of cosy.

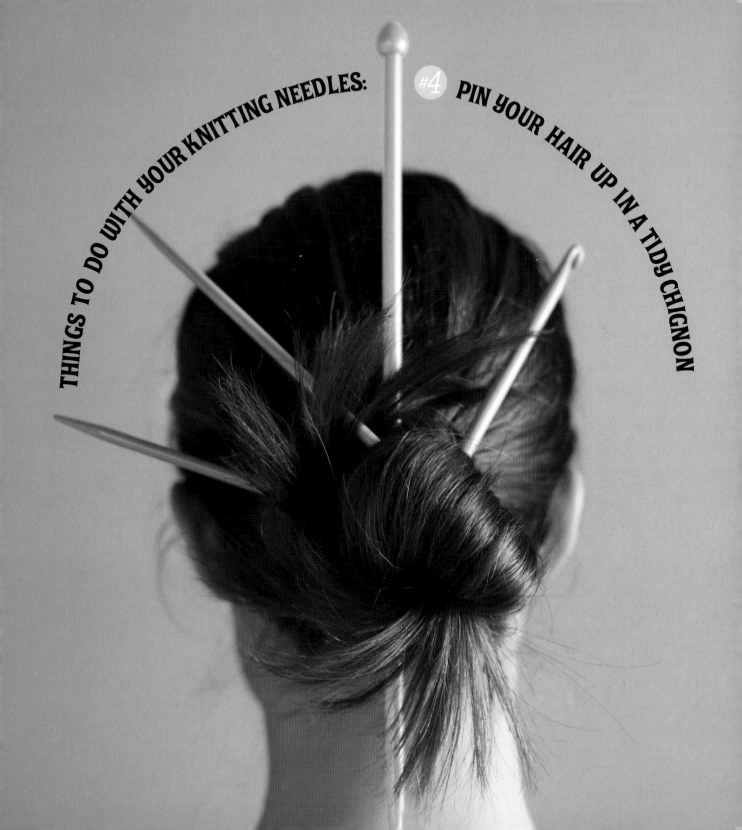

THINGS TO DO WITH YOUR KNITTING NEEDLES: #4 PIN YOUR HAIR UP IN A TIDY CHIGNON

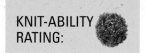
wine-bottle top

I saw this idea in an old knitting magazine and thought it would be great to give with a bottle of champagne or wine for an engagement party. The simple rib in this design makes it quick to knit up and the glitter in the wool provides a glamorous look.

#4 EXTREME KNITTING

Knitting on a camel...
sure to be a bumpy ride,
so watch those stitches!

MATERIALS — 1 x 50g ball of RYC Soft Lux.

NEEDLES — 1 pair of US 8 (5mm) needles.

GAUGE — 18 stitches and 24 rows to 4in/10cm square over stockinette stitch.

PATTERN

Cast on 50 stitches.

Row 1: Knit 1, *purl 4, knit 4* to last stitch, purl 1. Repeat row 1, 28 more times.

Bind off.

TO MAKE UP

Join side seam using mattress stitch (see page 31). Make two small pom-poms (see page 40). Using the central binding yarn, attach to top of side seam.

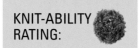
coasters

These are always a good thing to have around during parties and would make an ideal house-warming present, especially if your buddies have just bought new tables!

MATERIALS 1 x 50g ball Rowan Handknit Cotton DK in each of 3 shades A, B, and C will make approx. 24 circular or triangular coasters in various stripes.

NEEDLES 1 pair of US 7 (4.5mm) needles.

GAUGE 20 stitches and 28 rows to 4in/10cm square over stockinette stitch.

ABBREVIATIONS

M1: Make 1 stitch by picking up the strand between the stitch on the right-hand needle and the stitch on the left-hand needle and placing it on the left-hand needle, then knit into the back of it (see page 26).

PATTERN

Circular coasters
Using A cast on 12 stitches.
Row 1: Knit to end of row.
Row 2: Purl to end of row.
(These 2 rows form stockinette stitch.)
Row 3: Knit 1, M1, knit 10, M1, knit 1. (14 stitches).
Row 4: Purl to end of row.
Row 5: Knit 1, M1, knit 12, M1, knit 1. (16 stitches).
Row 6: Purl to end of row.

Join in B.
Row 7: Knit 1, M1, knit 14, M1, knit 1. (18 stitches).
Rows 8–12: Work in stockinette stitch.

Join in C.
Row 13: Knit 1, M1, knit 16, M1, knit 1. (20 stitches).
Row 14–16: Work in stockinette stitch.
Row 17: Knit 2 stitches together through the back of the stitches, knit to the last 2 stitches, knit 2 stitches together. (18 stitches)
Row 18: Purl to end of row.

Join in B.

Row 19: Knit 2 stitches together through the back of the stitches, knit to the last 2 stitches, knit 2 stitches together. (16 stitches).

Row 20: Purl to end of row.

Row 21: Knit 2 stitches together through the back of the stitches, knit to the last 2 stitches, knit 2 stitches together. (14 stitches).

Row 22: Purl to end of row.

Row 23: Knit 2 stitches together through the back of the stitches, knit to the last 2 stitches, knit 2 stitches together. (12 stitches).

Row 24: Purl to end of row.

Bind off.

Triangular coasters

Using A, cast on 5 stitches.

Row 1: Knit 1, M1, knit 3, M1, knit 1. (7 stitches).
Row 2: Purl to end of row.
Row 3: Knit 1, M1, knit 5, M1, knit 1. (9 stitches).
Row 4: Purl to end of row.
Row 5: Knit 1, M1, knit 7, M1, knit 1. (11 stitches).
Row 6: Purl to end of row.

Join in B.

Row 7: Knit 1, M1, knit 9, M1, knit 1. (13 stitches.)
Row 8: Purl to end of row.
Row 9: Knit 1, M1, knit 11, M1, knit 1. (15 stitches).
Row 10: Purl to end of row.
Row 11: Knit 1, M1, knit 13, M1, knit 1.
(17 stitches).
Row 12: Purl to end of row.

Join in C.

Row 13: Knit 1, M1, knit 15, M1, knit 1. (19 stitches).
Row 14: Purl to end of row.
Row 15: Knit 1, M1, knit 17, M1, knit 1. (21 stitches).
Row 16: Purl to end of row.
Row 17: Knit 1, M1, knit 19, M1, knit 1. (23 stitches).
Row 18: Purl to end of row.

Join in B.

Row 19: Knit 1, M1, knit 21, M1, knit 1. (25 stitches).
Row 20: Purl to end of row.
Row 21: Knit 1, M1, knit 23, M1, knit 1. (27 stitches).
Row 22: Purl to end of row.
Row 23: Knit 1, M1, knit 25, M1, knit 1. (29 stitches).
Row 24: Purl to end of row.

Bind off.

#4

WRAP GIFTS WITH IT!

glasses case

I felted this project to make it a bit sturdier—this case will hold either sunglasses or spectacles and you can even make some felted letters, for example a name, to sew onto the front of the case.

MATERIALS 1 x 100g ball of Rowan Big Wool Fusion.
1 x 50g ball of RYC Soft Tweed.

NEEDLES 1 pair of US 15 (10mm) needles.

GAUGE 10 stitches and 13 rows to 4in/10cm square over stockinette stitch using Big Wool fusion.

ABBREVIATIONS

MB (make bobble): (Knit 1, purl 1, knit 1) all into next stitch, turn needles and purl 3 stitches together, turn needles.

Turn: Swap needles, so work faces the other way.

PATTERN

Using Big Wool Fusion, cast on 23 stitches
Row 1: Knit to end of row.
Row 2: Purl to end of row.
(These 2 rows form stockinette stitch.)
Rows 3 and 4: Work in stockinette stitch.
Row 5: Knit 1, *MB, knit 1, repeat from * to end of row.
Rows 6–8: Work in stockinette stitch.

Row 9: Knit 2, *MB, knit 1, repeat from * to last stitch, knit 1.
Rows 10–12: Work in stockinette stitch.
Rows 13–20: As rows 5–12.
Bind off

TO ADD LETTERS

Using RYC Soft Tweed, cast on 20 stitches.
Row 1: Knit to end of row.
Row 2: Purl to end of row.
(These 2 rows form stockinette stitch.)
Work a further 16 rows in stockinette stitch.
Bind off.

To felt, put the pieces in separate pillow cases and machine wash at 140 degrees.

Leave to dry.

TO MAKE UP

Join side seams using mattress stitch.
Cut out your chosen letters and sew onto case using a matching color of thread.
Make handle by braiding 3 strands of Big Wool Fusion to measure 13½in/35cm. Sew one end to top of each side seam.

dice

When my best friend passed her driving test, I knitted her a pair of quirky wooly dice. Felting is so much fun to do and when you experiment with it, you can come up with some really interesting and fun designs.

MATERIALS 1 x 100g ball of Rowan Big Wool in each of two shades A and B.
Matching thread.
Polyester fiberfill (for stuffing).

NEEDLES 1 pair of US 17 (12mm) needles.

GAUGE 8 stitches and 11 rows to 4in/10cm square over stockinette stitch.

PATTERN

(Knit 1 piece from each ball.)
Cast on 20 stitches.
Continue in stockinette stitch to end of ball, leaving enough yarn to bind off.
Bind off.

To felt, put the pieces in separate pillow cases and machine wash at 140 degrees.
Once felted, leave to dry, then cut out 12 3x3in/8x8cm squares and 42 circles of each color.

TO MAKE UP

Sew circles on sides of dice with some matching thread. Sew squares together to form a cube, but before sewing the last side one, stuff the cube.

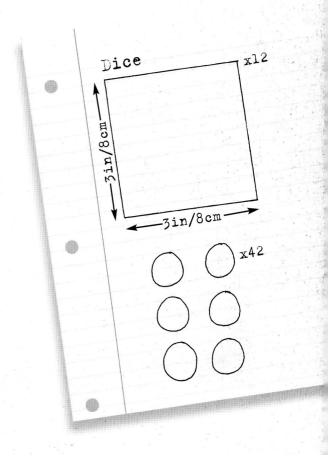

Louise's Knitted Cuff
(p110)

Amy's Corsage (p106)

Kate's Painted Tote Bag
(p118)

Suzie's Evening Purse
(p114)

customizing designs

At my knitting clubs I'm always looking for new inspiration or ways to inspire others. Customizing has become very popular recently in knitwear as more and more people become experimental and use this craft as an outlet for their creativity. So, I decided to brief five people who have either a textile, design, or fashion background to create a design using their particular skill as an inspiration, whether in customizing a basic knitted design or using a particular method of knitting.

In this chapter you will see that there are lots of ways of experimenting with this craft even if you are just a beginner, so please feel free to improvise and use your own skill and passion in your designs.

Di's Lacy Knitwear
(p122)

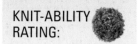

Amy's corsage

This is a funky corsage that reminds me of the 1920s, when everything was so elegant and sexy.

MATERIALS 1 x 25g ball of Rowan Yorkshire Tweed light. Wind into 2 balls.
1 x 50g ball of Rowan Lurex Shimmer.

NEEDLES 1 pair of US 7 (4.5mm) needles.

GAUGE 26 stitches and 38 rows to 4in/10cm square over stockinette stitch using Yorkshire Tweed yarn used in double thickness.

PATTERN

Using Yorkshire Tweed double, cast on 50 stitches.
Row 1: Knit to end of row.
Row 2: Purl to end of row.
Repeat the last 2 rows until there is enough yarn left to bind off.
Bind off.

TO MAKE UP

Put the piece of knitted fabric in the washing machine on a 140 degree wash (add detergent and an old towel to help agitate the knitting).
Reshape and dry flat.

Draw two different-sized petal-shaped templates and cut out five petals of each size. Pinching the larger ones at the bottom end, sew them together to create a flower shape. Add the smaller petals behind the larger ones in the gaps.

Add a circular piece of felt over the center of the flower to hide any stitching. Add further decoration if you like.

Once all petals have been sewn together, use some Rowan Lurex Shimmer and embroider around each petal. Add black ribbon to the back to create a rosette impression. Sew on a hairpin or broach pin.

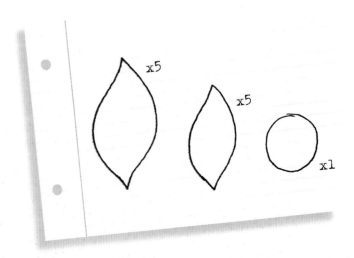

felted fun

The idea behind this design was to create something that was structured and three-dimensional.

NAME: Amy Gooda

AGE: 25

BACKGROUND: Constructed Textile Design, Gray's School of Art, Aberdeen.

MY STORY

I have always enjoyed creating structures and decorative forms and during my time at school I tried many different approaches to creating three-dimensional pieces. Since graduating I have spent a lot of time using my knitting machine to create fabric that has a three-dimensional element to it. Felting is something that I am still learning about as there are so many different techniques and finishes that can be achieved. At the moment I am still creating ideas and samples, trying various different approaches to see what works best for me.

MY INSPIRATION

I chose to create a felted flower because it meant I could create layers and make a structured form. This is much easier to do with felted pieces and I wanted to stick with a smaller project as you can see the results more quickly, ideal if this is your first attempt at felting. Also, because the piece is felted, it is much more robust and less likely to fall apart. It's also easier to customize—by adding some shimmering yarn and ribbon; you can make something very simple look fabulously sophisticated. Corsages are really versatile, you can pin it in your hair or on your clothes, or purse.

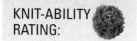
Louise's knitted cuff

This is a really simple design, but you can make the trimming as elaborate as you like—or design it to complement your own style.

MATERIALS 1 x100g ball of Rowan Big Wool in each of two shades.
12 Rowan buttons in different colors.
3 packets of Jaeger beads (in different colors).

NEEDLES 1 pair of US 15 (10mm) needles.

GAUGE 10 stitches and 13 rows to 4in/10cm square over stockinette stitch.

PATTERN

Cast on 20 stitches.
Work 16 rows in garter stitch (knitting every row), changing color as you wish.

TO MAKE UP

Sew 2 rows of 3 buttons on one short edge of the knitted piece to fasten the cuff together—just push the buttons through the knitting on the opposite edge.

Once the cuff is complete, customize the design using more buttons and add beads to join the button design.

#5 EXTREME KNITTING

Knitting on a hill top...
Let your surroundings
inspire you.

beaded jewels

I design wire-knitted jewelry, but here I chose to emphasize the knitted aspect and used buttons and beads as decoration.

NAME: Louise Pringle

AGE: 29

BACKGROUND: Constructed Textile Design, Heriot-Watt University.

MY STORY

A couple of years after I graduated from Heriot–Watt after studying Textile Design I showed a friend the work I had done for my degree show. I had made six final garments which incorporated knitted and beaded jewelry with wire at the neck and wrist areas, which I then graduated into the actual garment. It crossed the boundaries of clothing and jewelry. My friend took the garments into work and came back with 10 orders for knitted jewelry and wire cuffs. I now design different types of jewelry, which I sell in around 23 retailers, mostly in Scotland (www.eclecticshock.net).

MY INSPIRATION

I liked the idea of making an accessory that could be fastened to fit around any part of the arm, or even the ankle. In order for this to work it had to be adjustable. Thick wool knitted with big needles meant there were natural gaps in the knitting, big enough for average-sized buttons to be pushed through. I attached two rows of buttons on the edge of the knitted piece, which enabled the piece to be buttoned quite tightly around relatively large parts of the limb.

Suzie's evening purse

This is a really simple pattern, but the addition of the embroidery makes it stand out. You can sew your own design freehand, or trace the template overleaf, or use any other pattern you like.

MATERIALS
3 x 50g balls of RYC Cashsoft DK.
1 x 25g ball of Rowan Kidsilk Haze.
1 x 50g ball of Rowan Lurex Shimmer.
1 x 50g ball of Rowan Handknit Cotton DK.
1 pair of beaded handles.
2 metal snap fasteners.
Embroidery needles.

NEEDLES
1 pair of US 7 (4.5mm) needles.

GAUGE
22 stitches and 30 rows to 4in10cm square over stockinette stitch using Cashsoft DK.

PATTERN

Back and front (both alike)
Using Cashsoft DK, cast on 30 stitches
Row 1: Knit to end of row.
Row 2: Purl to end of row.
Rows 3–50: Repeat rows 1–2, 20 more times.
Bind off.

Gusset
Using Cashsoft DK, cast on 4 stitches.
Row 1: Purl to end of row.

Row 2: Knit 1, M1, knit to last stitch, M1, knit 1.
Row 3: Purl to end of row.
Row 4: Knit 2, M1, knit to last 2 stitches, M1, knit 2.
Rows 5–10: Repeat rows 3–4, 3 more times. (14 stitches).
Row 11: Purl to end of row.
Row 12: Knit to end of row.
Row 13: Purl to end of row.
Rows 14–79: Repeat rows 11–12, 33 more times.
Row 80: Knit 2, slip 1 stitch, pass slipped stitch over, knit to last 4 stitches, knit 2 stitches together, knit 2.
Row 81: Purl to end of row.
Rows 82–87: Repeat rows 80–81, 3 more times.
Row 88: Knit 1, slip 1 stitch, pass slipped stitch over, knit 2 stitches together, knit 1.
Row 89: Purl to end of row.
Bind off.

TO MAKE UP

Sew cast on and bind off edge of front and back to left and right side of gusset using mattress stitch. Embroider flower and leaf design using Kidsilk Haze, Lurex Shimmer, and Rowan Handknit Cotton DK.

Once finished, attach 2 beaded handles to side seams and add snap fasteners to the opening.

printed textile

Here, I've taken the concept of printing on textiles and transferred it to knitting and embroidery.

NAME: Suzie McGill

AGE: 25

BACKGROUND: Printed Textile Design, Edinburgh Art College, Heriot-Watt University.

MY STORY

I studied printed textile design where I regularly printed on various fabrics and wools. Embroidery is also important to me and is something I use a lot in my design work now. I've been interested in knitting ever since I began experimenting with different wools at art school and found that when I merged wool and print together I could come up with some different and unique designs. Knitting is a very relaxing and rewarding activity where you can create your own fabric to work onto: there are endless possibilities for experimenting.

MY INSPIRATION

My inspiration comes from nature, especially flowers, where ideas can be taken from the many colors, textures, and shapes.

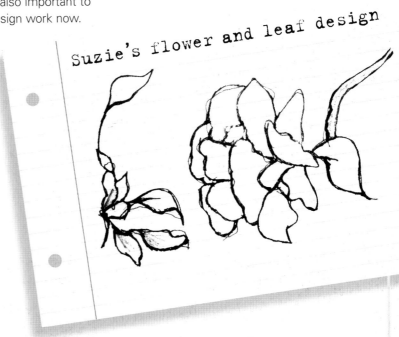

Suzie's flower and leaf design

Kate's painted tote bag

The sky's the limit—once you get the hang of charts, you can create your own design and knit your own cityscape onto this bag.

MATERIALS 3 x 50g balls of Rowan Handknit
Cotton DK in main color (M).
2 x balls in a contrasting color (C).
1 x 100g ball of Rowan Big Wool.

NEEDLES 1 pair each of size US 6 (4mm)
and US 15 (10mm) needles.

GAUGE 20 stitches and 28 rows to
4in/10cm square over stockinette
stitch using US 6 (4mm) needles
and Handknit Cotton DK.

PATTERN

Back
Using M and US 6 (4mm) needles, cast on 57
stitches
Row 1: Knit to end of row.
Row 2: Purl to end of row.
Rows 3–100: Repeat rows 1–2, 49 more times.
Bind off.

Front
Using M and US 6 (4mm) needles, cast on 57
stitches.
Work in pattern from chart (right).
Bind off.

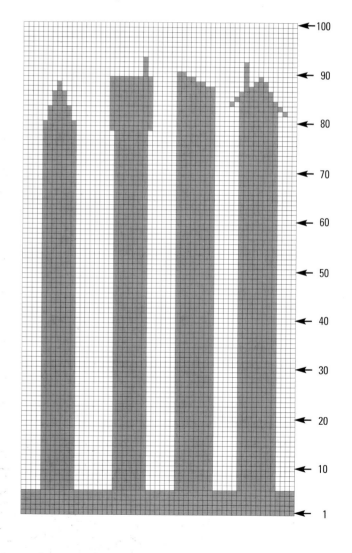

Handles (make 2)

Using US 15 (10mm) needles and Rowan Big Wool, cast on 10 stitches.

Row 1: Knit to end of row.
Row 2: Purl to end of row.
Rows 3–38: Repeat rows 1–2, 18 more times. Bind off.

TO MAKE UP

Embroider windows and lamppost onto front (see diagrams below). Join side seams. Sew on handles.

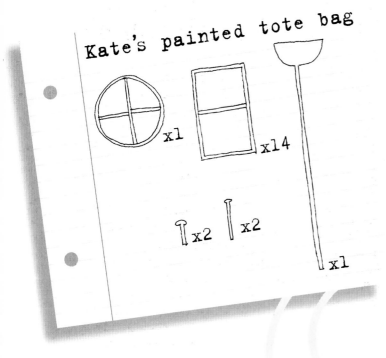

Kate's painted tote bag

x1 x14 x2 x2 x1

paint 'n' knit

Here I used one of my own paintings (far right) as inspiration for my knitted design.

NAME: Kate Green

AGE: 25

BACKGROUND: Design Futures, Napier University.

MY STORY

Color has always been a major part of my life; it gives me confidence and I use it to express my mood. I started painting with bright colors at school where I was encouraged to be more free and expressive, experimenting with shapes and different media. I then went on to do a degree in Design Futures where I got out of the habit of painting, concentrating more on graphics and computer-aided design. After school I traveled through Eastern Europe, North Africa, and Australia and it wasn't until I returned to Scotland that I got back into painting. I think a part of me is rebelling against computers and the

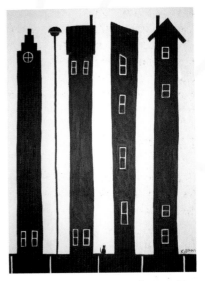

modern age, as when you are painting you are not relying on any sort of technology, you have more freedom to express your mood, and each painting is original and unique.

MY INSPIRATION

I am inspired by Scotland—its small coastal villages, the Highlands, and particularly Edinburgh's Old Town with its towering tenements, narrow alleyways, and crowded buildings. I am also inspired by contrasting color patterns, which I feel is reflected in my artwork. I like to knit in my spare time and my paintings inspire the colors of wool I use, which is why I decided to use one of my paintings as a design for a bag. (www.kategreenartist.co.uk)

Di's lacy knitwear

I lined the panty with silk and added some frilly lace elastic—you could also add crazy amounts of ribbon and lace for a girly, pretty feel.

MATERIALS 2 x 50g balls of Rowan Kid Classic.

NEEDLES 1 pair of US 7 (4.5mm) needles.

GAUGE 20 stitches and 25 rows to 4in/10cm square over stockinette stitch.

ABBREVIATIONS

M1: Make 1 stitch by picking up the strand between the stitch on the right-hand needle and the stitch on the left-hand needle and placing it on the left-hand needle, then knit into the back of it.

YF: Bring yarn forward between needles, then take it over the right-hand needle to make 1 stitch.

PATTERN

Front
Cast on 16 stitches.
Row 1: Knit to end of row.
Row 2: Purl twice in first stitch, purl to last stitch, purl twice in last stitch. (18 stitches).
Row 3: Knit to end of row.
Rows 4 and 5: As rows 2 and 3. (20 stitches).
Row 6: Purl twice in first stitch, purl to last stitch, purl twice in last stitch. (22 stitches).
Row 7: Knit twice in first stitch, knit to last stitch,

knit twice in last stitch. (24 stitches).
Rows 8–10: Repeat rows 6 and 7 once more, then row 6 again. (30 stitches).
** Row 11: Cast on 5 stitches, knit to end of row.
Row 12: Cast on 5 stitches, purl to end. (40 stitches).
Row 13: Knit 1, *knit 2 stitches together, YF, knit 1, repeat from * to last 3 stitches, knit 3.
Row 14: Cast on 3 stitches, purl to end of row.
Row 15: Cast on 3 stitches, knit to end. (46 stitches).
Row 16: Cast on 6 stitches, purl to end of row.
Row 17: Cast on 6 stitches, knit 6, *knit 2 stitches together, YF, knit 1, repeat from * to last stitch, knit 1. (58 stitches).
Row 18: Cast on 5 stitches, purl to end of row.
Row 19: Cast on 5 stitches, knit to end. (68 stitches).
Row 20: Cast on 7 stitches, purl to end of row.
Row 21: Cast on 7 stitches, knit 8, *knit 2 stitches together, YF, knit 1, repeat from * to last 2 stitches, knit 2. (82 stitches).
Row 22: Purl to end of row.
Row 23: Knit to end of row.
Row 24: Purl to end of row.
Row 25: Knit 1, *knit 2 stitches together, YF, knit 1, repeat from * to last 3 stitches, knit 3.
Row 26: Purl 2 stitches together, purl to last 2 stitches, purl 2 stitches together. (80 stitches).
Row 27: Knit to end of row.
Row 28: Purl 2 stitches together, purl to last 2 stitches, purl 2 stitches together. (78 stitches).

Rows 29–44: Repeat rows 25–28, 4 more times. On each repetition of row 25, work the lace repeat to the last 1, 2, or 3 stitches as appropriate, then knit these last stitches. (62 stitches).

Row 45: *Knit 1, purl 1, repeat from * to end of row.

Rows 46–48: Repeat row 45, 3 more times.

Bind off.

Back

Cast on 30 stitches.

Purl 1 row.

Work as given for Front from ** to end.

Gusset

Cast on 30 stitches.

Row 1: Knit to end of row.

Row 2: Knit to end of row.

Row 3: Purl to end of row.

Row 4: Knit 1, slip 1, knit 1, pass slipped stitch over last knitted stitch, knit to last 3 stitches, knit 2 stitches together, knit 1.

Row 5: As row 3.

Rows 6–21: Repeat rows 4–5, 8 more times. (12 stitches).

Repeat rows 2–3 twice more.

Row 26: Knit 1, M1, knit to last stitch, M1, knit 1. (14 stitches).

Repeat row 3, then rows 2–3.

Row 30: As row 26. (16 stitches).

Row 31: Purl to end of row.

Row 32: Knit to end of row.

Row 33: Knit to end of row.

Bind off.

TO MAKE UP

Using mattress stitch, join cast on and bind off edges of gusset to cast on edges of front and back (be careful to sew through cast on and bound off gusset stitches, above knitted ridge). Join side seams using mattress stitch.

lacy knitwear

Why panties? Because I think knitting is so feminine and the lacy panty really expresses this.

NAME: Diana Kiernander

AGE: 28

BACKGROUND: MA Fashion, London College of Fashion.

MY STORY

I'm a writer and fashion stylist really, but I enjoy knitting as it's the perfect way to relax and keep busy at the same time! Since I started knitting I've experimented greatly! Knitted nightgowns, men's jackets, puffball skirts, and now the panties. Wool is wonderful for anyone with imagination. Once you've mastered the basics I honestly don't think there's anything that can't be knitted! I knit a lot in cafés and it's interesting to watch people's reaction. You get a few funny looks, but most people want to chat. They reminisce about knitting or tell you about their dog! I think knitting must be comforting to watch. No one feels threatened by a knitter, that's for sure.

MY INSPIRATION

I believe fashion is a fantasy and this feeling influences all of my work. At the same time, people who don't follow fashion but have instead their own style impress me. Strong, independent women who are super-feminine inspire my work. And I like to recall the past in my work—I think this design is certainly nostalgic. The idea of knitted panties is a little bizarre but there's a femininity about them, through the lace detail, that makes them appealing. I didn't expect anyone to want to wear these panties at first but there's been a lot of interest. Maybe because it's so cold in the winter here! Though I reckon they'd look good in summer, too, maybe worn as a bikini. You'd certainly stand out on the beach! (www.elfieloves.com)

index

acknowledgments

This book has been the best thing I've ever worked on. I've loved every minute of it and I'm so grateful I was given the opportunity by Kyle Cathie to do such a project with a team of such creative and enthusiastic people who have made this book complete and were also a pleasure to work with: my editor, Muna Reyal; my book designer, Jenny Semple; my photographer, Kate Whitaker; my models Amy Redmond, Jenny and Laura Wheatley, and Jacob Love; my pattern writer Penny Hill; my illustrator, Roberta Boyce; my knitters Reinhilde Van Den Brande and my mom; as well as my friends who contributed designs to my book: Kate, Diana, Louise, Suzie, and Amy, not forgetting Rowan Yarns for all their gorgeous yarn!

I would also like to thank the many inspirational and talented people whom I've met over the past few years, as well as those who currently surround me in my knitted world, without whom I would not be so inspired and driven: Sharon Brant, Debbie Abrahams, Kate Buller, Jeanette Trottman, Carol Meldrum, fellow students at Lauder College, Gray's School of Art, all the pub knitters at Sofis and, most of all, my family.

Thank you and happy knitting!

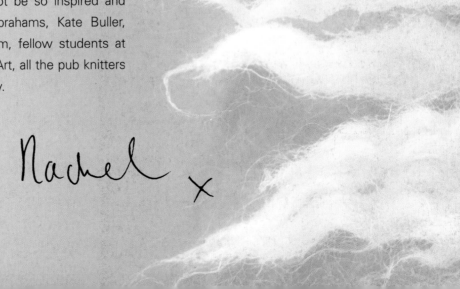